THE EYE OF THE WHALE

A Rescue Story

For Lulu Delacre, Susan Stockdale, and Janet Morgan Stoeke—with love and gratitude for your invaluable assistance with this book. And in memory of Ruby, my loyal companion for fourteen years.

I thank James Moskito, who was so generous in giving his time to tell me his story. I also thank Mick Menigoz for kindly allowing me to go on his boat, *Superfish*, to the Farallon Islands. Thanks also to Kathi Koontz for sharing further details on the rescue.   —JO'C.

A portion of the author's proceeds from the sale of this book goes to support the work of The Marine Mammal Center in Sausalito, California, www.MarineMammalCenter.org.

TILBURY HOUSE PUBLISHERS
12 Starr Street
Thomaston, Maine 04861
800–582–1899 • www.tilburyhouse.com

First paperback printing March 2016
ISBN 978-0-88448-395-3
10 9 8 7 6 5 4

Library of Congress Cataloging-in-Publication Data
O'Connell, Jennifer, 1956-
  The eye of the whale : a rescue story / Jennifer O'Connell. — First hardcover edition.
    pages cm
  Audience: K to grade 3.
  ISBN 978-0-88448-335-9 (hardcover : alk. paper)
 1. Humpback whale—California—San Francisco—Juvenile literature. 2. Wildlife rescue—California—San Francisco—Juvenile literature. I. Title.
  QL737.C424O26 2012
  599.5'25—dc23   2012031165

Designed by Geraldine Millham, Westport, Massachusetts
Printed and bound in Korea

THE EYE OF THE WHALE

A Rescue Story

Jennifer O'Connell

TILBURY HOUSE PUBLISHERS · THOMASTON, MAINE

*T*hrough the morning fog, a fisherman sees trouble.

It's a whale—tangled in the lines from crab traps.
"Whale in distress!" he calls into his radio.

Back on shore a captain answers the call.
"We're on it," he says.

The captain assembles his rescue team. James, a dive master, has never been close to a whale. He doesn't know what to expect.

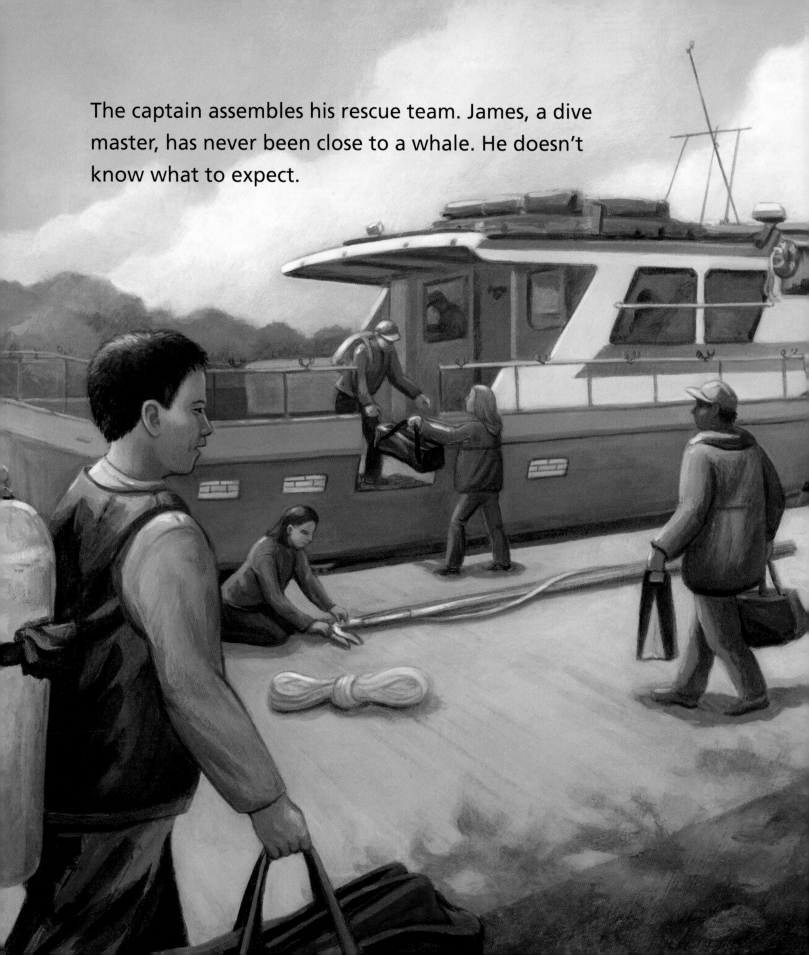

They might not reach the whale in time.
Sharks could find it first.

When they reach the reported location, there is only a sea lion, bobbing in the waves. Then a puff of mist shoots up.
The captain speeds over.

The whale is floating, not moving. It is huge, most likely a female. "Can't see much below the surface," says the captain. James puts on his flippers.

"We're going in," James says.
"Be careful of the tail," warns the captain.

The divers rise and fall with the dark swells.
Water churns as the whale rolls to her side.

An eye slowly surfaces and looks at James.
Then a giant flipper appears and James
knows to stay back.

The whale rolls down again and James swims
to her side. He sees lines cutting into her skin.
He takes a deep breath and dives.

There are scores of ropes trapping the whale.

The divers race back to the boat.
"We have to cut the lines or she'll die!" James shouts.

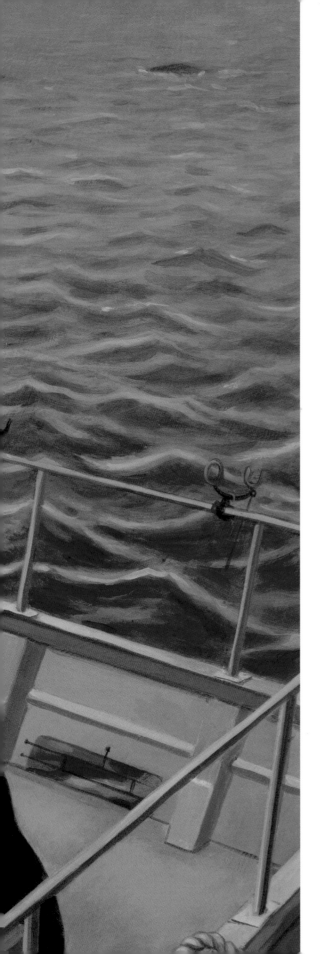

"She swims with her tail, so we'll cut those lines last. If the whale starts moving, get out of the way!"

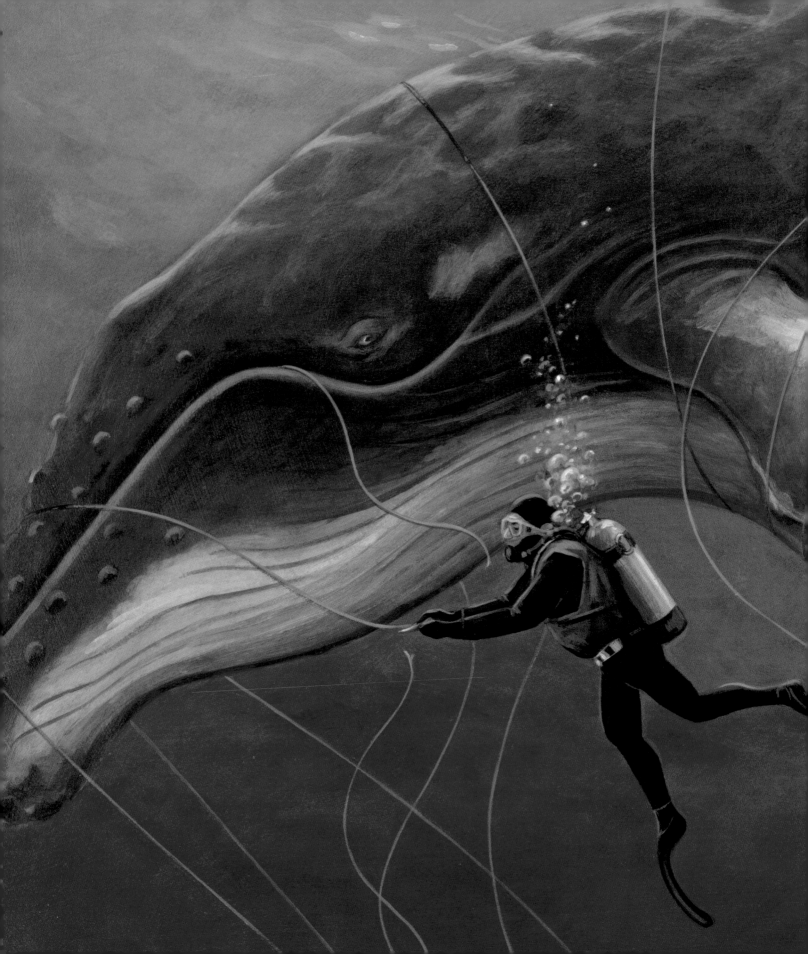

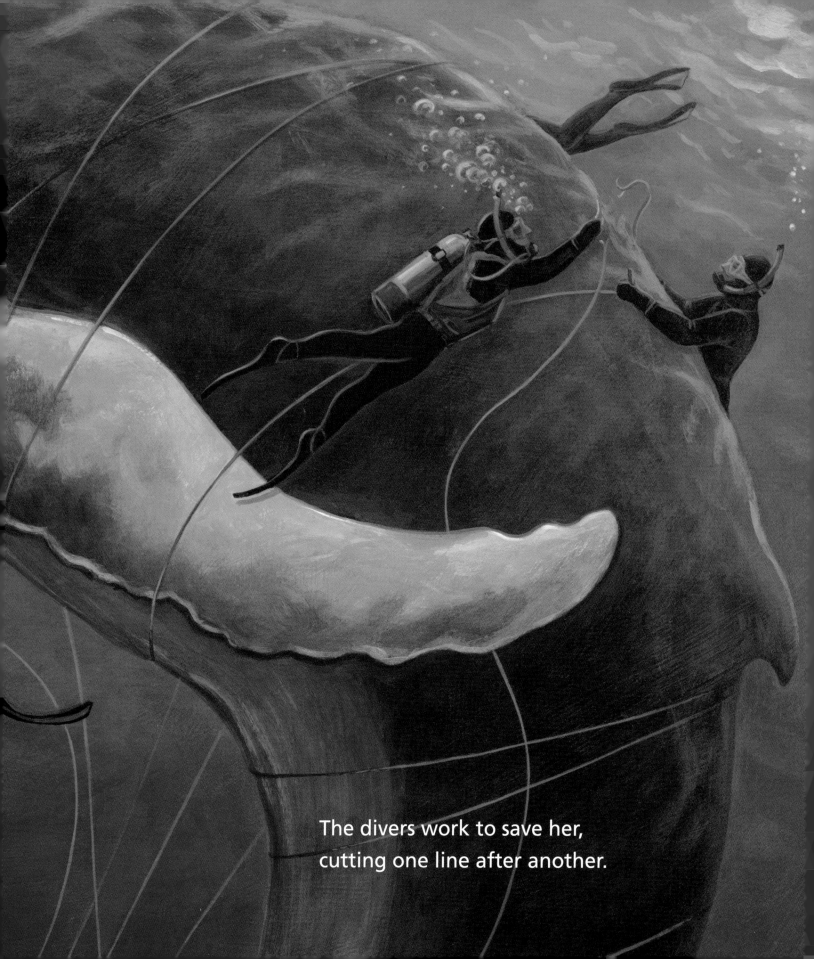

The divers work to save her,
cutting one line after another.

The whale watches everything James does.

Finally, the last line is cut and the whale drifts down into the deep water.

"We did it!" The divers scan the ocean for movement. They know the whale must come up to breathe. James wonders where she has gone. Then a loud humming sound vibrates through the water.

And they see her. The whale whirls around the divers in a fast, wild dance. Then she disappears. James is puzzled.

With a jolt, James sees her heading straight for him!

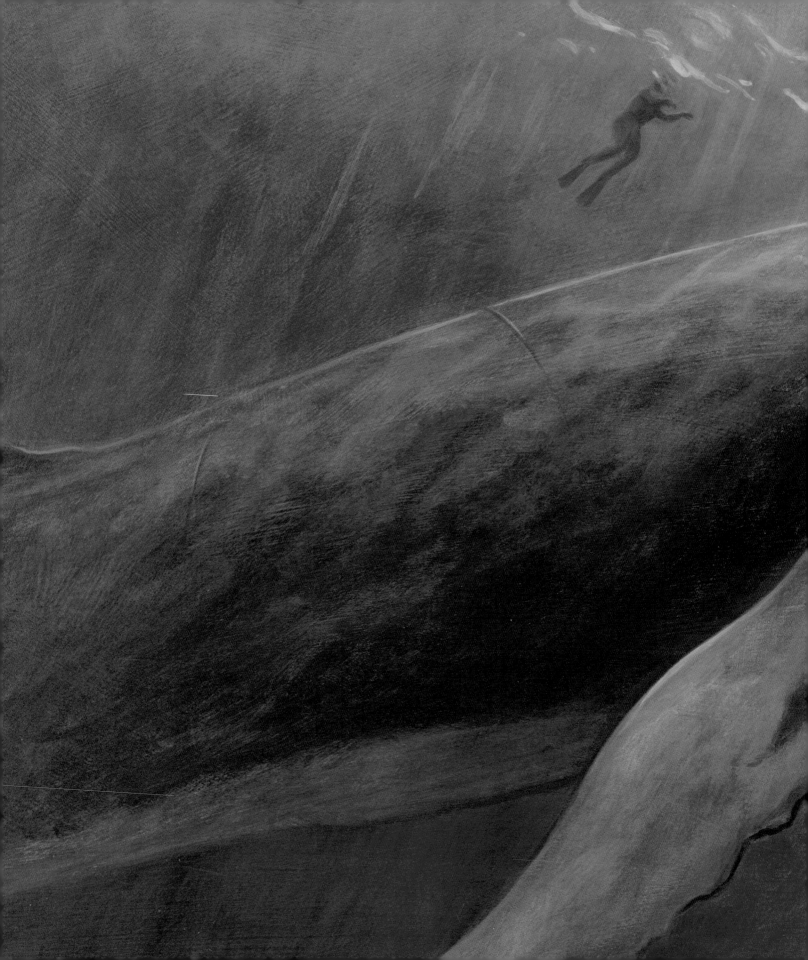

The whale pushes him, ever so gently, a little nudge.
Then, one by one, she nudges the other divers, too.

She looks at James with her beautiful eye.
And plunges back into the dark sea.

On the morning of December 11, 2005, fisherman Ryan Tom came upon a 50-foot-long humpback whale tangled in crab-trap lines about 18 miles off the coast of San Francisco.

He called Captain Mick Menigoz, who then called The Marine Mammal Center, an organization that helps mammals that live in the ocean. The rescue crew rushed to Captain Mick's boat, *Superfish*, and they set off to see what could be done.

When the crew found the whale, she was barely able to keep her blowhole above the surface to breathe. Hundreds of yards of tangled lines and heavy crab traps were anchoring the whale down to the ocean floor. Realizing how hard it would be to cut lines from on board the boat, divers James Moskito, Tim Young, Jason Russey, and Ted Vivian went into the water to cut them. They were risking their lives, since one quick move of a whale's tail can kill a person (which, sadly, has occurred in the past). Others on board *Superfish* included Dr. Frances Gulland, DVM, Jim Smith, and Kathi Koontz, all fromThe Marine Mammal Center, as well as crew members Geary Barnes and Holly Drouillard. The story quickly spread and has been celebrated around the world.

As people found out about the event, questions arose. Did the whale help the divers by staying still and calm as they cut the lines, or was she just exhausted? Was the whale full of joy after being freed, or did she swim in circles to stretch out her huge body after being tied up for so long? How do we explain the whale nudging all the divers, then looking directly at each of them?

Research on whale brains suggests that whales may have the ability to experience emotions. We don't know what this particular whale was feeling. What we do know is that the rescue had a great emotional impact on the divers, who said that when the whale swam up to them and nudged them, it was one of the most fantastic moments of their lives.

Humans continue to kill whales with hunting, pollution, boat propellers, fishing lines, nets, and sonar. If we choose to respect and protect these magnificent creatures, they will continue to live and inspire future generations.

About Humpback Whales

Humpbacks live in family groups called pods. They are unique among whales for their long, bumpy flippers—in fact, the flippers give the whale its scientific name, *Megaptera novaeangliae*, which means "Big-winged New Englander." They are found in all the world's oceans except the Arctic, usually near the coast. They can live 50 years and grow as big as a school bus, weighing 40 tons. Humpback whales summer in the high-latitude waters of the North Atlantic, North Pacific, and Southern oceans where food is plentiful, and winter in tropical waters for mating and calving. Their seasonal migrations can cover more than 3,000 miles (5,000 kilometers).

Humpbacks are baleen whales. To feed they take in great mouthfuls of water, so much that their pleated throats expand, and strain it out through the curtain of flexible baleen that hangs down from their upper jaw. They then swallow the fish, krill, and other small creatures that remain in their mouths. An adult whale eats up to 1.5 tons (1,350 kilograms) of food each day.

Humpback whales can dive, or *sound,* for up to 30 minutes, reaching depths up to 700 feet (210 meters). They can also *breach,* or leap clear of the water—a truly impressive sight that is never forgotten by anyone who sees it.

The males make complex "songs" that can be heard up to 20 miles away and may be a part of mating behavior. How they do this without vocal cords is still not known. You can find recordings of these hauntingly beautiful songs online.

In 2006, scientists Patrick Hof and Estel Van Der Gucht of the New York Consortium in Evolutionary Primatology made an important discovery. They found spindle cells in a humpback whale's brain. Until then, spindle cells were known to exist only in the brains of humans and great apes. In humans, spindle cells are responsible for self-awareness, social interaction, and the processing of emotions. In larger whales, these cells are found in the same parts of the brain as in humans—areas that regulate emotional functions such as social organization, empathy, speech, intuition, and instinctive responses.

Large whales have up to three times the number of spindle cells as humans and have been evolving these cells for 30 million years—twice as long as humans. Does this mean that they are more advanced and smarter than we are? Scientists don't know, nor do they know if the emotions that we humans feel are the same as those in the great whales. But we do know that large whales have acted in ways that reflect intelligence and suggest a deep emotional capability, as witnessed during the rescue featured in this book.

Kevin O'Connell

Jennifer O'Connell is the bestselling author and illustrator of the picture book *Ten Timid Ghosts,* the author of *It's Halloween Night!* and the illustrator of *A Garden of Whales,* among others. A two-time recipient of the Christopher Award, Jennifer also creates illustrations for book covers and magazines.

To research *The Eye of the Whale,* Jennifer traveled to San Francisco, where she met Captain Mick Menigoz and rode his rescue boat, *Superfish,* out into the Pacific Ocean to the area where the events in the book took place. This experience fueled her inspiration as she created the images and words of this extraordinary story.

Jennifer lives with her husband, Kevin, in Bethesda, Maryland, and speaks frequently about her books and the bookmaking process. Visit her online at www.JenniferOConnellArt.com.